Customized Learning Developing Special Education Curriculum for Individual Needs

Charlotte

Title: Customized Learning Developing Special Education Curriculum for Individual Needs

Author's: Charlotte.

This book was printed and published by [Publisher's: Charlotte] in [2023]

ISBN:

TABLE OF CONTENTS

Chapter 1: Understanding Special Education Curriculum Development

Introduction to Special Education Curriculum

In today's diverse society, it is crucial to ensure that every learner has access to an education that meets their unique needs. This is especially true for students with special needs, who may require additional support and accommodations to thrive academically. The field of special education has been developed to address these needs and provide a tailored curriculum that promotes their individual growth and development.

The purpose of this subchapter is to introduce the concept of special education curriculum and its importance in meeting the needs of students with disabilities. Whether you are a teacher, administrator, parent, or anyone interested in curriculum development, this subchapter aims to provide you with a foundational understanding of special education curriculum and its significance in promoting inclusive education.

Special education curriculum refers to the specific instructional materials, strategies, and methods designed to meet the learning goals and objectives of students with disabilities. Unlike a one-size-fits-all approach, special education curriculum takes into account the unique strengths, challenges, and learning styles of each individual student. It is tailored to address their specific needs, whether they have learning disabilities, autism spectrum disorder, intellectual disabilities, or other exceptionalities.

The development of special education curriculum requires collaboration among educators, administrators, parents, and other stakeholders to create a comprehensive plan that addresses the diverse needs of students. It involves assessing individual students' strengths and weaknesses, setting appropriate goals, and selecting instructional strategies that are research-based and evidence-informed.

The subchapter will explore the key components of special education curriculum, including individualized education plans (IEPs), accommodations and modifications, assistive technology, and differentiated instruction. It will also delve into best practices for curriculum development, such as inclusive practices, Universal Design for Learning (UDL), and culturally responsive teaching.

By the end of this subchapter, you will have a solid understanding of what special education curriculum entails and its role in promoting inclusive education. You will be equipped with knowledge and strategies to develop and implement effective curriculum plans that cater to the unique needs of students with disabilities. Whether you are an educator looking to enhance your teaching practice or an administrator seeking to create an inclusive learning environment, this subchapter will provide you with the tools and insights necessary to support the academic success of every learner.

The Importance of Individualized Learning

In the realm of education, one size does not fit all. Every student is unique, with their own abilities, strengths, and challenges. Hence, it is imperative for educators and curriculum developers to embrace individualized learning to ensure that every learner reaches their full potential. This subchapter explores the significance of individualized learning in curriculum development and its profound impact on students.

Individualized learning is a teaching approach that tailors instruction to meet the specific needs of each student. It recognizes that students have different learning styles, interests, and paces of learning. By personalizing the curriculum, educators can engage students more effectively and create a positive and inclusive learning environment.

One of the primary benefits of individualized learning is that it promotes student engagement and motivation. When students are actively involved in their own learning, they become more interested and invested in the subject matter. This fosters a love for learning and helps students develop a lifelong passion for education.

Furthermore, individualized learning allows students to progress at their own pace. By recognizing their strengths and weaknesses, educators can provide targeted support and resources to help students overcome challenges and excel in areas where they are already proficient. This personalized approach prevents students from feeling overwhelmed or bored and ensures that they are continuously challenged and motivated to learn.

Individualized learning also promotes inclusivity and equity in education. Students with diverse learning needs, such as those with special education requirements, benefit greatly from personalized instruction. By adapting the curriculum to their individual needs, educators can provide a level playing field for all students, allowing them to thrive academically and emotionally.

Lastly, individualized learning prepares students for the real world. In today's rapidly evolving society, adaptability and critical thinking skills are paramount. By customizing learning experiences, students develop these essential skills, enabling them to navigate challenges and succeed in their future careers.

In conclusion, individualized learning is crucial in curriculum development, benefiting all students, regardless of their learning style or abilities. It fosters student engagement, motivates learners, promotes inclusivity, and equips students with the skills needed for success in the real world. As educators and curriculum developers, it is our responsibility to embrace individualized learning and create an educational system that caters to the diverse needs of every learner.

Legal and Ethical Considerations in Special Education Curriculum Development

In the field of special education, developing a curriculum that meets the individual needs of every student is of utmost importance. However, it is equally essential to consider the legal and ethical aspects that govern this process. Understanding and adhering to these considerations ensures that curriculum development aligns with the rights and well-being of all students. This subchapter aims to provide an in-depth analysis of the legal and ethical considerations in special education curriculum development.

Legal considerations form the foundation of any curriculum development process. Special education is governed by federal laws such as the Individuals with Disabilities Education Act (IDEA). This legislation outlines the rights of students with disabilities and requires schools to provide them with a free and appropriate education. Curriculum development must take into account the specific needs and goals identified in each student's Individualized Education Program (IEP) to ensure compliance with IDEA. Additionally, other federal laws, such as Section 504 of the Rehabilitation Act and the Americans with Disabilities Act (ADA), protect the rights of individuals with disabilities and require schools to make reasonable accommodations to meet their needs.

Ethical considerations are equally important in special education curriculum development. Educators must uphold ethical principles that ensure fairness, respect, and equality for all students. The principles of non-discrimination, inclusion, and cultural responsiveness guide the development of a curriculum that acknowledges and values the diverse backgrounds and abilities of students. Ethical guidelines also emphasize the importance of informed consent from parents or guardians and the active involvement of students in the decision-making process regarding their education.

Furthermore, ethical considerations extend to the design of instructional materials and assessment methods. Curriculum developers must ensure that materials are accessible and inclusive to students with various disabilities. This may involve providing alternative formats, incorporating assistive technology, or employing Universal Design for Learning (UDL) principles. Assessment methods must also be fair and appropriate, taking into account the individualized goals and abilities of students.

By considering both the legal and ethical aspects of special education curriculum development, educators can create an inclusive and supportive learning environment for all students. This subchapter aims to provide guidance and practical strategies for curriculum developers, teachers, and administrators to navigate these considerations effectively. By doing so, we can ensure that the curriculum is not only tailored to individual needs but also upholds the legal rights and ethical principles that underpin special education.

Chapter 2: Assessing Individual Needs

Individualized Education Program (IEP) Process

The Individualized Education Program (IEP) process is a critical component in ensuring that students with special needs receive the appropriate education and support to meet their individualized goals. This subchapter will provide an overview of the IEP process, its significance in curriculum development, and its impact on individual student success.

The IEP process is a collaborative effort that involves various stakeholders, including parents, teachers, special education professionals, and school administrators. It begins with the identification of a student's unique needs through assessments, evaluations, and observations. These findings are then used to develop specific goals and objectives tailored to the student's strengths, challenges, and learning style.

Curriculum development plays a vital role in the IEP process as it guides the selection of instructional strategies, materials, and resources that best support the student's individual needs. By customizing the curriculum, educators can differentiate instruction, modify content, and adapt teaching methods to ensure that students with special needs have equal access to education.

The IEP process also emphasizes the importance of ongoing assessment and progress monitoring. Regular evaluations are conducted to assess the student's progress towards their goals, identify areas of improvement, and make necessary adjustments to the curriculum. This continuous feedback loop ensures that the student's educational plan remains relevant and effective.

Furthermore, the IEP process promotes the inclusion of transition goals for students nearing the end of their schooling journey. These goals focus on preparing students for life beyond the classroom, including post-secondary education, employment, and independent living. By incorporating transition planning into the IEP process, educators can equip students with the necessary skills and resources to successfully transition into adulthood.

It is crucial for educators, parents, and all stakeholders to actively participate in the IEP process. Collaboration and open communication between all parties are key to developing an effective and individualized education plan. By working together, we can create an inclusive and supportive learning environment that promotes the academic, social, and emotional growth of every student.

In conclusion, the IEP process is a cornerstone of curriculum development for students with special needs. It ensures that their education is tailored to their unique strengths and challenges, promoting their overall development and success. By understanding and actively participating in the IEP process, educators can make a significant impact on the lives of students with special needs, fostering a culture of customized learning that embraces diversity and individuality.

Conducting Assessments for Special Education Students

In the realm of special education, assessments play a vital role in developing effective and customized curriculum for students with individual needs. These assessments provide valuable insights into the strengths and weaknesses of students, enabling educators and curriculum developers to tailor educational experiences that promote inclusive learning and optimal growth.

Assessments for special education students are multifaceted and comprehensive, encompassing various domains such as academic, cognitive, social-emotional, and behavioral aspects. The purpose of these assessments is to identify students' unique learning styles, preferences, and challenges, ultimately guiding the design of curriculum that caters to their specific needs.

One commonly used assessment tool is the Individualized Education Program (IEP). The IEP is a personalized plan that outlines the student's academic goals, accommodations, and modifications necessary for their success. However, developing an effective IEP requires a thorough understanding of the student's abilities and limitations. This is where assessments come into play.

Academic assessments are an essential component of determining a student's current level of knowledge and skills. These evaluations can include standardized tests, informal observations, and performance-based assessments. By identifying academic gaps and areas of strength, educators can design curriculum that targets the specific skills the student needs to develop.

Cognitive assessments, on the other hand, delve into a student's cognitive functioning, including their intellectual abilities, memory, attention, and problem-solving skills. These assessments provide valuable insights into a student's learning potential and cognitive strategies. Armed with this information, educators can employ instructional techniques that align with the student's cognitive strengths, fostering a more effective and engaging learning experience.

Social-emotional and behavioral assessments are equally important for special education students. These assessments help identify any emotional or behavioral challenges that may impact the student's learning and social interactions. By understanding these factors, educators can implement appropriate strategies, interventions, or supports to ensure that the student's emotional well-being is addressed, creating an environment conducive to learning.

Conducting assessments for special education students is a critical aspect of curriculum development. It allows educators and curriculum developers to gain a comprehensive understanding of the student's unique needs, strengths, and challenges. Armed with this knowledge, they can create tailored curriculum that promotes inclusive learning and maximizes the student's potential.

In conclusion, assessments are the cornerstone of developing effective and customized curriculum for special education students. By utilizing various assessment tools, educators can gain insights into academic, cognitive, social-emotional, and behavioral aspects, allowing for the creation of personalized curriculum that meets the needs of each individual student. Through these assessments, educators can ensure that every student receives an inclusive and meaningful educational experience.

Understanding Different Types of Assessments

Assessments play a crucial role in curriculum development, especially in the realm of special education where individual needs must be carefully addressed. In this subchapter, we will explore the various types of assessments used to evaluate students' progress and tailor educational plans to their individual needs. Whether you are a teacher, parent, or educational professional, understanding these different assessment methods will empower you to create a customized learning experience that maximizes the potential of every student.

1. Diagnostic Assessments: These assessments are conducted at the beginning of the learning process to identify students' strengths, weaknesses, and prior knowledge. Diagnostic assessments provide valuable insights into individual students' needs, allowing educators to design appropriate interventions and support.

2. Formative Assessments: Formative assessments are ongoing evaluations that monitor students' progress throughout a learning unit or project. These assessments provide real-time feedback to both teachers and students, enabling them to make necessary adjustments and improvements. Formative assessments promote personalized learning experiences by identifying areas where additional support or enrichment is required.

3. Summative Assessments: Summative assessments are typically administered at the end of a learning unit or course to evaluate students' overall understanding and mastery of the content. These assessments often take the form of exams, projects, or presentations. Summative assessments provide a comprehensive view of students' progress and help determine if learning goals have been achieved.

4. Authentic Assessments: Authentic assessments focus on real-world applications and require students to demonstrate their knowledge and skills through practical tasks or projects. These assessments encourage critical thinking, problem-solving, and creativity, providing a holistic view of students' abilities beyond traditional tests and exams.

5. Portfolio Assessments: Portfolio assessments involve the collection of students' work samples over a period of time, showcasing their growth and development. This method allows educators to examine students' progress across various learning areas and provides a comprehensive view of their abilities, strengths, and areas for improvement.

By understanding and utilizing these different types of assessments, curriculum developers can create individualized learning plans that address the unique needs of every student. Whether it is identifying areas for improvement, providing ongoing support, or evaluating overall progress, assessments are integral to developing a customized learning experience in special education. By incorporating a variety of assessment methods, educators can ensure that students receive the support and opportunities they need to thrive academically and develop essential skills for life beyond the classroom.

Chapter 3: Designing Individualized Learning Goals

Setting Meaningful and Measurable Goals

Setting meaningful and measurable goals is an essential aspect of curriculum development, particularly in the field of special education. In order to provide individualized instruction that meets the unique needs of students, educators must be able to identify and track progress towards specific learning objectives. This subchapter will explore the importance of setting meaningful and measurable goals, and provide practical strategies for doing so effectively.

Meaningful goals are those that are relevant and significant to the individual student. They should align with the student's abilities, interests, and long-term aspirations. By setting goals that are meaningful to the student, educators can foster a sense of personal investment and motivation, which greatly enhances the learning experience. For example, a student with a passion for art may set a goal to develop their artistic skills and create a portfolio of their work.

Measurable goals are those that can be quantified or observed in a concrete manner. They provide a clear framework for assessing progress and determining whether the desired outcomes have been achieved. Measurable goals also allow for effective communication and collaboration between educators, parents, and other stakeholders involved in the student's educational journey. For instance, a measurable goal for a student with a reading disability may be to improve their reading fluency by 20 words per minute within a specific timeframe.

To set meaningful and measurable goals, educators can employ a variety of strategies. Firstly, they should conduct a comprehensive assessment of the student's abilities, strengths, and areas for improvement. This assessment may include formal testing, informal observations, and input from the student and their parents or guardians. Based on this assessment, educators can collaboratively establish goals that are challenging yet attainable for the student.

Additionally, educators should ensure that goals are broken down into smaller, manageable steps. This allows for incremental progress and builds confidence in the student. Regular monitoring and evaluation of progress towards these goals is crucial, as it allows for timely adjustments and interventions as needed.

In conclusion, setting meaningful and measurable goals is a fundamental aspect of curriculum development in special education. By establishing goals that are relevant and significant to the individual student, educators can foster motivation and engagement. Measurable goals provide a clear framework for assessment and communication, facilitating effective collaboration between all stakeholders. By employing strategies such as comprehensive assessment, breaking goals into smaller steps, and regular monitoring, educators can ensure that students receive individualized instruction that meets their unique needs.

Incorporating Standards and Benchmarks

In the realm of curriculum development, the incorporation of standards and benchmarks holds great significance. When it comes to special education, this aspect becomes even more crucial as it ensures that students with individual needs receive a comprehensive and tailored education.

Standards serve as a framework that outlines the knowledge, skills, and abilities that students should acquire at each grade level. They provide a roadmap for educators, helping them design curriculum and instruction that aligns with broader educational goals. By incorporating standards into special education curriculum development, educators can ensure that students with individual needs are not left behind and have access to the same educational opportunities as their peers.

To effectively incorporate standards into special education curriculum, it is essential to recognize the unique needs of each student. Special education students often require customized instruction and support to meet their individual learning goals. By identifying the specific standards relevant to each student, educators can create a curriculum that is both meaningful and challenging.

Benchmarks, on the other hand, serve as checkpoints along the educational journey. They provide a way to measure progress and determine whether students are meeting the desired standards. By incorporating benchmarks into special education curriculum development, educators can track students' growth and make necessary adjustments to ensure their success.

When developing a specialized curriculum for special education students, it is important to consider a range of factors beyond academic standards. Individualized Education Programs (IEPs) play a crucial role in addressing the unique needs of each student. By aligning IEP goals with standards and benchmarks, educators can create a more integrated and comprehensive curriculum that caters to the diverse needs of special education students.

Incorporating standards and benchmarks into special education curriculum development also promotes accountability. It allows educators to demonstrate that students with individual needs are making progress and meeting educational standards. This not only benefits the students but also enhances the credibility of the special education program as a whole.

In conclusion, the incorporation of standards and benchmarks is a vital aspect of special education curriculum development. By aligning curriculum with standards and utilizing benchmarks to measure progress, educators can ensure that students with individual needs receive a quality education that prepares them for success in the broader educational landscape. Through this holistic approach, special education students can thrive and reach their fullest potential.

Addressing Unique Learning Styles and Abilities

In the realm of education, one size does not fit all. Every student possesses unique learning styles and abilities that must be acknowledged and accommodated for effective curriculum development. This subchapter delves into the concept of addressing these individual needs and provides insights into customized learning strategies for diverse learners.

Understanding the diverse learning styles and abilities of students is crucial for effective curriculum development. This knowledge enables educators to design specialized instructional approaches that cater to the specific needs of each student. By acknowledging and addressing these unique learning styles and abilities, educators can create an inclusive and supportive learning environment that promotes the success of all students.

One of the key aspects of addressing unique learning styles and abilities is recognizing that students learn in different ways. Some students may be visual learners, who grasp concepts better through images and visual aids. Others may be auditory learners, who benefit from listening to lectures or discussions. There are also kinesthetic learners, who learn best through hands-on activities and physical engagement. By incorporating a variety of instructional methods, educators can ensure that all students have equal opportunities to understand and absorb the curriculum.

Additionally, addressing unique learning styles and abilities involves identifying and accommodating for students with exceptional abilities. Gifted students, for instance, require educational experiences that challenge and stimulate their advanced intellectual capabilities. By providing accelerated learning opportunities, enrichment programs, or individualized projects, educators can foster the growth and development of these exceptional learners.

Moreover, addressing unique learning styles and abilities can involve utilizing assistive technology and adaptive strategies. Assistive technologies such as text-to-speech software, screen readers, or visual aids can significantly enhance the learning experience for students with disabilities, enabling them to access and comprehend the curriculum more effectively. Adaptive strategies, such as breaking down complex concepts into smaller, more manageable parts, can also support students with learning difficulties or cognitive impairments.

In conclusion, addressing unique learning styles and abilities is a fundamental aspect of curriculum development. By recognizing and accommodating for diverse learning styles and abilities, educators can create an inclusive and effective learning environment that caters to the needs of all students. Through the incorporation of various instructional methods, accommodations for exceptional learners, and the use of assistive technology, customized learning can be achieved, ensuring that every student has an equal opportunity to succeed.

Chapter 4: Adapting Instructional Strategies

Differentiating Instruction for Special Education Students

In the field of education, it is widely recognized that no two students are the same. Each student has unique strengths, weaknesses, and learning styles. For students with special education needs, it becomes even more crucial to provide instruction that is tailored to their individual needs. This subchapter aims to delve into the concept of differentiating instruction for special education students, offering insights and strategies for curriculum development that will benefit both educators and learners.

Differentiating instruction refers to the practice of adapting teaching methods, materials, and assessments to meet the diverse needs of students. In the context of special education, this approach becomes even more critical. By recognizing and addressing the specific learning difficulties, disabilities, or exceptionalities of each student, educators can create a more inclusive and effective learning environment.

One key aspect of differentiating instruction for special education students is the identification of individualized education goals. It is essential to assess and understand the unique needs and abilities of each student, enabling educators to develop personalized learning objectives. By setting realistic and attainable goals, educators can provide focused instruction that caters to the specific challenges and strengths of each learner.

Furthermore, differentiating instruction involves adapting teaching strategies and materials to suit various learning styles. Special education students may require alternative methods of instruction, such as visual aids, hands-on activities, or technology-enhanced materials. By incorporating these diverse approaches into the curriculum, educators can engage students more effectively and enhance their learning experience.

Another crucial aspect of differentiating instruction is the use of flexible assessments. Traditional assessments may not effectively capture the progress and achievements of special education students. Educators should consider alternative assessment methods, such as performance-based assessments, portfolios, or verbal evaluations, which provide a more comprehensive understanding of a student's abilities.

Moreover, collaboration and communication between educators, special education professionals, and families play a crucial role in differentiating instruction. By sharing information and insights about a student's needs, progress, and challenges, these stakeholders can work together to develop effective and individualized learning plans.

In conclusion, differentiating instruction for special education students is an essential aspect of curriculum development. By recognizing and addressing the unique needs of these learners, educators can create a more inclusive and effective learning environment. Through individualized education goals, adapted teaching strategies and materials, flexible assessments, and collaborative efforts, special education students can receive the personalized instruction they need to thrive academically and holistically.

Utilizing Assistive Technology in Curriculum Development

In today's rapidly evolving world, the field of education is constantly seeking innovative ways to cater to the diverse learning needs of students. One effective approach that has gained significant attention is the utilization of assistive technology in curriculum development. This subchapter aims to explore the potential of integrating assistive technology into educational practices, specifically focusing on its impact on curriculum development.

Assistive technology refers to any tool or device that helps individuals with disabilities to enhance their learning experiences and overcome obstacles that may hinder their academic progress. By incorporating assistive technology into curriculum development, educators can create a more inclusive and accessible learning environment for all students.

The benefits of utilizing assistive technology in curriculum development are vast. Firstly, it promotes personalized learning by adapting the curriculum to meet the individual needs of each student. Assistive technology tools such as text-to-speech software, speech recognition programs, or alternate input devices enable students with reading or writing difficulties to actively engage with the curriculum content. This customization empowers students to learn at their own pace and style, leading to improved academic outcomes.

Moreover, assistive technology fosters independence and self-advocacy in students with disabilities. By providing them with tools that compensate for their challenges, students can actively participate in classroom activities and take ownership of their learning journey. This not only boosts their confidence but also equips them with vital skills needed for their future endeavors.

Incorporating assistive technology in curriculum development also encourages collaboration among students. With the aid of communication tools, students can engage in group discussions, share ideas, and collaborate on projects more effectively. This inclusive learning environment promotes empathy, understanding, and respect among students with and without disabilities.

However, it is crucial to acknowledge that the successful integration of assistive technology in curriculum development requires proper training and support for educators. Providing teachers with professional development opportunities and access to resources will enable them to effectively incorporate assistive technology into their lesson plans, ensuring its seamless integration with the curriculum.

In conclusion, the utilization of assistive technology in curriculum development has the potential to revolutionize education and create a more inclusive learning environment. By personalizing learning experiences, promoting independence, fostering collaboration, and supporting diverse learning needs, assistive technology can significantly enhance the academic journey of students with disabilities. It is imperative for educators and curriculum developers to embrace this transformative approach and equip themselves with the necessary tools and knowledge to harness the power of assistive technology.

Modifying Classroom Environment and Resources

In the field of curriculum development, it is crucial to recognize the unique needs of every learner, especially when it comes to special education. Customized Learning: Developing Special Education Curriculum for Individual Needs is dedicated to addressing these needs and providing educators with practical strategies to create an inclusive and supportive learning environment.

One key aspect of developing an effective special education curriculum is modifying the classroom environment. The physical space should be designed in a way that encourages engagement, collaboration, and independence for all students. Flexible seating arrangements, adaptive furniture, and various sensory tools can be incorporated to cater to different learning styles and abilities. Additionally, visual aids, such as charts, schedules, and labels, can help students with organization and understanding of expectations.

Creating a positive and inclusive classroom culture is equally important. Educators should foster a sense of belonging, respect, and acceptance among all students. This can be achieved through promoting open communication, encouraging peer collaboration, and celebrating individual strengths and achievements. By valuing diversity and creating a safe and supportive environment, students will feel empowered to engage actively in their learning.

Moreover, modifying classroom resources is essential to meet the individual needs of special education students. Traditional print materials can be supplemented with digital resources, assistive technologies, and multimedia tools. These resources can provide alternative modes of instruction, reinforce concepts, and offer opportunities for independent practice. Additionally, educators should adapt materials by using simplified language, visual supports, or tactile elements to enhance comprehension and accessibility.

Another aspect to consider is the differentiation of instructional strategies. As educators, it is important to employ a variety of teaching methods and approaches to accommodate diverse learning profiles. This may involve using multisensory techniques, hands-on activities, or individualized instruction. Differentiated instruction allows students to access the curriculum at their own pace and in a way that best suits their learning preferences and abilities.

In conclusion, modifying the classroom environment and resources is crucial in developing a special education curriculum that meets the individual needs of students. By creating an inclusive and supportive learning environment, educators can optimize student engagement, collaboration, and independence. Additionally, adapting classroom resources and differentiating instructional strategies can further enhance accessibility and provide opportunities for personalized learning experiences. By customizing the learning environment and resources, educators can empower every student to reach their full potential.

Chapter 5: Creating Accessible Learning Materials

Designing Adapted Materials for Students with Disabilities

In the realm of education, it is crucial to provide inclusive and equitable learning opportunities for all students, including those with disabilities. These students often require adapted materials that cater to their individual needs and learning styles. This subchapter aims to explore the process of designing and implementing adapted materials for students with disabilities, ensuring that they receive a customized learning experience that fosters their academic and personal growth.

The development of adapted materials begins with a comprehensive understanding of the specific disabilities and unique requirements of each student. This knowledge enables curriculum developers to design materials that accommodate their cognitive, physical, sensory, or emotional challenges. By doing so, educators can create an inclusive environment that promotes active participation and maximizes learning outcomes.

Designing adapted materials involves various considerations. First and foremost, it is essential to align the content with the student's individualized education program (IEP) goals and objectives. This ensures that the materials directly address their educational needs and facilitate progress towards their desired outcomes. Additionally, materials should be designed with flexibility in mind, allowing for modifications and accommodations as necessary. This flexibility allows educators to tailor the materials to meet the unique learning needs of each student.

Moreover, the accessibility of adapted materials is of utmost importance. Consideration should be given to font size, color contrast, and readability to accommodate students with visual impairments. For those with hearing impairments, providing captions or sign language interpretations may be necessary. Furthermore, materials should be presented in multiple formats, such as braille or audio, to cater to students with different learning styles and preferences.

Collaboration between educators, special education professionals, and the students themselves is crucial throughout the design process. By involving all stakeholders, educators can gain invaluable insights into the specific needs and preferences of the students. This collaboration ensures that the adapted materials truly meet the individual requirements and foster a sense of ownership and empowerment among students.

In conclusion, designing adapted materials for students with disabilities is a vital aspect of curriculum development. By considering individual needs, aligning with IEP goals, and ensuring accessibility, educators can create a customized learning experience that caters to the unique requirements of each student. Through collaboration and inclusivity, we can provide an equitable education for all students, fostering their academic success and personal growth.

Incorporating Universal Design for Learning (UDL) Principles

Universal Design for Learning (UDL) is an educational framework that promotes inclusive and flexible teaching practices to meet the diverse needs of all learners. By integrating UDL principles into curriculum development, educators can create a learning environment that caters to individual needs, fostering academic success and personal growth for every student.

The concept of UDL is based on the idea that learners have unique strengths, preferences, and challenges. To address this diversity, UDL emphasizes the provision of multiple means of representation, engagement, and expression. By offering various ways to access and demonstrate knowledge, educators can remove barriers to learning and empower students to reach their full potential.

Incorporating UDL principles into curriculum development begins with identifying the specific needs of the target audience. By considering the range of abilities, learning styles, and preferences within a classroom, educators can design instruction that accommodates everyone. This may involve providing different formats of instructional materials, such as text, audio, or visuals, to ensure that all students can engage with the content effectively.

UDL also encourages the use of flexible instructional strategies that allow for individualized learning experiences. By offering choices and options, educators can cater to diverse learning preferences and engage students in a meaningful way. This may involve providing opportunities for hands-on activities, peer collaboration, or incorporating technology to enhance learning.

Furthermore, UDL promotes the use of assessment methods that value diverse modes of expression. Traditional assessments often focus on written exams or standardized tests, which may not accurately reflect the knowledge and skills of all students. By offering alternative assessment methods, such as presentations, projects, or multimedia creations, educators can allow students to demonstrate their understanding in ways that align with their strengths and preferences.

Incorporating UDL principles into curriculum development not only benefits students with special needs but also enhances the learning experience for all learners. By embracing inclusivity and providing multiple means of engagement, representation, and expression, educators can create a dynamic and engaging learning environment that promotes success for every student.

By adopting UDL principles, curriculum developers can ensure that their materials and instructional strategies are accessible and meaningful to a diverse range of learners. Whether designing curriculum for special education settings or mainstream classrooms, integrating UDL principles can lead to more effective and inclusive instruction, benefiting both educators and students alike.

Ensuring Accessibility in Digital Learning Resources

In today's digital age, accessibility is a key consideration when developing learning resources for students with special needs. The use of digital tools and resources has opened up new possibilities for personalized and customized learning experiences. However, it is crucial to ensure that these resources are accessible to all students, regardless of their abilities or disabilities. This subchapter aims to explore various strategies and best practices for ensuring accessibility in digital learning resources, with a specific focus on curriculum development.

One of the first steps in ensuring accessibility is to design digital resources with universal design principles in mind. Universal design promotes the creation of products and environments that are usable by all people, to the greatest extent possible, without the need for adaptation or specialized design. By applying these principles, curriculum developers can ensure that digital resources are accessible to students with diverse needs, including those with visual, hearing, or cognitive impairments.

Another important aspect of accessibility in digital learning resources is the use of assistive technology. Assistive technology includes a wide range of tools and devices that help individuals with disabilities to perform tasks that they would otherwise have difficulty completing. For example, screen readers can assist visually impaired students in accessing text-based content, while captioning and transcripts can make audio and video resources accessible to students with hearing impairments.

Additionally, it is essential to provide multiple means of representation, engagement, and expression in digital learning resources. This means offering content in various formats, such as text, audio, and visual, to accommodate different learning styles and preferences. Furthermore, interactive elements, such as quizzes, simulations, and games, can enhance student engagement and provide opportunities for active learning and participation.

Ensuring accessibility also involves considering the compatibility of digital resources with different devices and platforms. It is important to develop resources that can be accessed on a variety of devices, including desktop computers, laptops, tablets, and smartphones. Moreover, compatibility with different operating systems and assistive technologies should be taken into account to ensure seamless access to the resources.

In conclusion, ensuring accessibility in digital learning resources is crucial for providing inclusive and equitable educational opportunities for all students. By adhering to universal design principles, leveraging assistive technology, offering multiple means of representation and engagement, and considering compatibility, curriculum developers can create accessible resources that cater to the diverse needs of students with special needs. By embracing accessibility in digital learning, we can empower every student to reach their full potential and participate fully in the educational journey.

Chapter 6: Collaborating with Parents and Caregivers

Building Effective Partnerships with Families

In the realm of curriculum development, it is crucial to recognize the significance of building effective partnerships with families. Families play a vital role in the education and development of children, particularly those with special education needs. By fostering strong relationships and collaboration with families, educators can create a supportive and inclusive learning environment that caters to the individual needs of each student.

One of the key aspects of building effective partnerships with families is open and consistent communication. Regular communication channels should be established, allowing for ongoing dialogue between educators and families. This communication should not only be limited to discussing academic progress but also involve sharing concerns, victories, and any other relevant information. By keeping families informed and involved, they feel valued and become active participants in their child's educational journey.

Furthermore, educators should seek to understand and respect the unique cultural backgrounds and perspectives of each family. Recognizing and celebrating diversity can greatly enhance the partnership between families and educators. By incorporating cultural knowledge into the curriculum, educators can create a more inclusive and engaging learning experience for all students.

Collaboration is another essential element in building effective partnerships with families. Educators should actively seek input from families and involve them in the decision-making process. By including families' insights and perspectives, educators can gain a deeper understanding of the student's individual needs and tailor the curriculum accordingly. This collaborative approach ensures that the curriculum is customized to meet the specific requirements of each student, maximizing their learning potential.

Building effective partnerships with families also involves providing resources and support. Educators should strive to offer families access to relevant information, training, and tools that can assist them in supporting their child's educational journey. By empowering families with knowledge and resources, educators enable them to become effective advocates for their child's education, ensuring their needs are met both inside and outside of the classroom.

In conclusion, building effective partnerships with families is a fundamental aspect of curriculum development, particularly in special education. By establishing open communication, respecting cultural diversity, fostering collaboration, and providing resources and support, educators can create a truly inclusive and personalized learning experience for students. These partnerships enable families to actively contribute to their child's education and ensure that their individual needs are met, ultimately leading to improved academic outcomes and overall well-being.

Engaging Parents in the Curriculum Development Process

In the pursuit of providing quality education to all students, it is essential to involve parents in the curriculum development process. Parents play a crucial role in their child's education, and their input and collaboration can greatly enhance the effectiveness of the curriculum. This subchapter explores the significance of engaging parents in the curriculum development process and provides practical strategies for curriculum developers to involve parents effectively.

Why Engage Parents in Curriculum Development?

Parents are the primary advocates for their children and possess valuable insights into their child's strengths, weaknesses, and individual needs. By involving parents in the curriculum development process, educators can gain a deeper understanding of the diverse needs of the students they serve. Parents bring a unique perspective that can help identify any gaps in the existing curriculum and suggest modifications or additions that would better serve their child's educational requirements.

Furthermore, engaging parents in curriculum development fosters a sense of ownership and empowerment among parents. When parents feel involved and valued in the education of their children, they are more likely to actively participate in their child's learning journey, leading to improved academic outcomes.

Strategies for Engaging Parents in Curriculum Development

1. Establish Open Communication Channels: Create an open and welcoming environment where parents feel comfortable sharing their ideas, concerns, and suggestions. This can be achieved through regular parent-teacher meetings, surveys, and feedback forms.

2. Collaborative Decision-Making: Involve parents in decision-making processes by seeking their opinions and involving them in discussions related to curriculum development. Encourage them to contribute their expertise and experiences, as this will help create a curriculum that is relevant and responsive to the needs of individual students.

3. Parent Workshops and Training: Conduct workshops and training sessions to familiarize parents with the curriculum development process. This will enable them to better understand the objectives, content, and teaching strategies employed in the curriculum, enabling them to provide more informed feedback.

4. Parent Representation in Curriculum Committees: Include parent representatives in curriculum committees to ensure their voices are heard and considered during the decision-making process. This will give parents a platform to actively contribute to the development and evaluation of the curriculum.

By actively involving parents in the curriculum development process, educators can create a more inclusive, tailored, and effective curriculum that meets the diverse needs of every student. When parents and educators collaborate, they form a powerful partnership that can positively impact the educational experiences and outcomes of all students.

Supporting Parent Advocacy for Individualized Learning

In the realm of education, one size does not fit all. Each student has unique needs, strengths, and interests that must be taken into account to ensure their success. This is especially true for students with special education needs, who require an individualized approach to learning. However, creating a customized curriculum can be a complex task, and it is essential to have the support of parents and caregivers to ensure the best possible outcomes for these students.

Parent advocacy plays a critical role in promoting and supporting individualized learning for students with special needs. Parents are the experts when it comes to their child's abilities, challenges, and learning styles. They possess valuable insights that can greatly contribute to the development of a personalized curriculum. By actively involving parents in the curriculum development process, educators can tap into this wealth of knowledge and ensure that the educational plan truly reflects the unique needs of the student.

One way to support parent advocacy is through open and ongoing communication. Regular meetings, such as parent-teacher conferences or individual education plan (IEP) meetings, provide opportunities for parents to share their observations, concerns, and goals for their child's education. These discussions can help educators gain a deeper understanding of the student's strengths and challenges, enabling them to tailor the curriculum accordingly. By actively listening to parents and valuing their input, educators can foster a collaborative partnership that benefits the student.

Another way to empower parent advocacy is by providing them with resources and information. Many parents of children with special needs may feel overwhelmed and unsure of how to navigate the education system. Educators can offer guidance on available support services, assistive technologies, and strategies for promoting learning at home. By equipping parents with the necessary knowledge and tools, they can become effective advocates for their child's individualized learning.

Furthermore, educators can encourage parent involvement through workshops and training sessions. These opportunities can educate parents about the principles of individualized learning, the importance of ongoing assessment, and strategies for supporting their child's unique needs. By fostering a shared understanding between educators and parents, the curriculum development process becomes a collaborative effort that leads to more effective and meaningful learning experiences for the student.

In conclusion, supporting parent advocacy is crucial for the success of individualized learning. By actively involving parents in the curriculum development process, educators can tap into their expertise and gain valuable insights. Open communication, providing resources, and offering training opportunities are all ways to empower parents to become effective advocates for their child's education. When parents and educators work together, they can create a customized curriculum that meets the unique needs of each student with special needs, ultimately leading to improved learning outcomes.

Chapter 7: Evaluating and Monitoring Progress

Using Data to Measure Student Growth

In the field of education, it is crucial to monitor and measure student growth accurately. By doing so, educators can identify areas of improvement, tailor instruction, and provide targeted interventions to ensure every student reaches their fullest potential. This subchapter explores the importance of using data to measure student growth and how it can be effectively utilized in curriculum development for special education.

Data-driven decision-making is a powerful tool that enables educators to make informed choices about instructional strategies, curriculum design, and individualized interventions. By collecting and analyzing various types of data, such as standardized test scores, formative assessments, behavioral observations, and progress monitoring, educators can gain valuable insights into student performance and progress.

The first step in utilizing data to measure student growth is establishing clear and measurable learning goals. These goals should be specific, measurable, attainable, relevant, and time-bound (SMART). When educators set SMART goals for students, it becomes easier to track their progress and adjust instruction accordingly.

Once learning goals are established, educators can collect data through a variety of methods. Standardized tests provide a valuable snapshot of student performance and can be used to compare growth over time. Formative assessments, on the other hand, provide immediate feedback on student understanding and can be used to adjust instruction on a daily basis. Behavioral observations and progress monitoring tools, such as checklists and rubrics, can help capture non-academic aspects of student growth, such as social-emotional development and behavior.

Analyzing and interpreting the collected data is the next crucial step. Educators must look for patterns, trends, and areas of improvement to inform their instruction. This analysis can provide insights into individual student needs, identify gaps in the curriculum, and guide the development of targeted interventions.

Finally, data should be used to inform curriculum development for special education. By analyzing student performance data, educators can identify areas where the curriculum needs to be modified or adapted to meet individual needs. This customization ensures that students receive the support and instruction necessary for their growth and success.

In conclusion, using data to measure student growth is paramount in curriculum development for special education. By setting SMART goals, collecting various types of data, analyzing patterns, and using the insights to adapt instruction, educators can provide the necessary support for every student. Data-driven decision-making empowers educators to make informed choices and create a personalized learning experience that caters to individual needs, ultimately leading to improved student outcomes.

Implementing Formative and Summative Assessments

Formative and summative assessments play a crucial role in the development and evaluation of special education curriculum for individual needs. These assessment methods provide valuable insights into students' progress, strengths, and areas of improvement, enabling educators to tailor instruction to meet their unique requirements. In this subchapter, we will explore the importance of implementing both formative and summative assessments in the curriculum development process.

Formative assessments are ongoing evaluations that help educators track student performance and understanding throughout the learning process. By using a variety of formative assessment strategies such as quizzes, observations, and class discussions, teachers can gather real-time feedback and make immediate adjustments to their instructional strategies. These assessments provide students with an opportunity to reflect on their learning, identify areas of weakness, and seek additional support if needed. Formative assessments not only guide instruction but also foster a growth mindset, encouraging students to view mistakes as opportunities for growth.

On the other hand, summative assessments are typically administered at the end of a unit, semester, or school year to evaluate students' overall learning and mastery of concepts. These assessments provide a comprehensive view of students' progress and enable educators to make informed decisions regarding promotion, graduation, or further interventions. Summative assessments, such as standardized tests, portfolios, or projects, provide a summation of a student's accomplishments and provide valuable data for program evaluation and accountability.

Integrating formative and summative assessments in curriculum development ensures that educators have a holistic understanding of students' strengths, challenges, and progress. By employing formative assessments, educators can identify gaps in knowledge and adjust instruction in real-time, ensuring that students receive the necessary support and interventions. Additionally, summative assessments provide a comprehensive evaluation of students' learning outcomes, enabling educators to evaluate the effectiveness of instructional strategies and make data-driven decisions for future curriculum development.

To effectively implement formative and summative assessments, educators should consider various factors, such as the individual needs of students, assessment validity and reliability, and alignment with curriculum goals and standards. Moreover, it is essential to provide students with clear expectations and rubrics to ensure fairness and transparency in the assessment process.

In conclusion, formative and summative assessments are integral components of customized learning in special education. By implementing these assessment methods, educators can gain valuable insights into students' learning progress, tailor instruction to their individual needs, and evaluate the effectiveness of the curriculum. By using a combination of formative and summative assessments, educators can create a supportive and inclusive learning environment that empowers students to reach their full potential.

Analyzing Progress and Making Instructional Adjustments

In the journey of customized learning and developing special education curriculum for individual needs, one crucial aspect that cannot be overlooked is the continuous analysis of progress and the subsequent adjustments in instructional strategies. This subchapter aims to provide insights into the importance of analyzing progress and making necessary adjustments to ensure effective curriculum development in the field of special education.

Analyzing progress is an essential component of any curriculum development process, as it helps educators and stakeholders to determine the effectiveness of the instructional strategies being employed. By closely monitoring the progress of students, educators can identify areas of strength and weakness, enabling them to make informed decisions about the curriculum. This analysis helps in tailoring the curriculum to meet the individual needs of students, ensuring that they receive the most appropriate and effective education.

Furthermore, analyzing progress also allows educators to identify any gaps or discrepancies in the curriculum. It provides an opportunity to reevaluate the goals and objectives set for students and make necessary adjustments to bridge those gaps. This process ensures that the curriculum remains dynamic and responsive to the changing needs of each student, making it more inclusive and effective.

Making instructional adjustments based on the analysis of progress is crucial to ensure that students receive the support they need to succeed. These adjustments may involve modifying teaching strategies, incorporating additional resources, or providing individualized instruction. By tailoring instruction to address specific learning needs, educators can optimize student engagement and enhance learning outcomes.

Curriculum development professionals, educators, and stakeholders in the field of special education will greatly benefit from understanding the significance of analyzing progress and making instructional adjustments. This knowledge empowers them to create a curriculum that is adaptable, responsive, and effective in meeting the diverse needs of students with special educational needs.

In conclusion, analyzing progress and making instructional adjustments are essential aspects of curriculum development in special education. By closely monitoring progress, educators can identify areas for improvement and make necessary adjustments to ensure that the curriculum is responsive to individual needs. This subchapter serves as a guide for curriculum development professionals and educators, enabling them to create customized learning experiences that empower students with special educational needs to reach their full potential.

Chapter 8: Adapting the Curriculum Over Time

Continuously Assessing and Modifying Individualized Learning Plans

In the realm of education, the concept of individualized learning plans has gained significant traction in recent years. Recognizing that each student has unique strengths, challenges, and learning styles, educators have embraced the idea of tailoring instruction to meet individual needs. However, creating an individualized learning plan is just the beginning. To ensure its effectiveness, it is essential to continuously assess and modify these plans.

Assessment is a key component of any educational endeavor, and individualized learning plans are no exception. Regularly assessing students' progress allows educators to gauge their understanding, identify areas of improvement, and make informed decisions about modifying the learning plan. This ongoing evaluation helps ensure that students are receiving the support they need and are making steady progress towards their educational goals.

There are various assessment strategies that can be employed to monitor the effectiveness of individualized learning plans. These may include formative assessments, such as quizzes or discussions, that provide immediate feedback on student understanding. Summative assessments, such as exams or projects, can also be used to evaluate overall progress. Additionally, informal methods like observations and student self-reflections can provide valuable insights into the effectiveness of the learning plan.

Modifying individualized learning plans based on assessment data is crucial to address the evolving needs of students. As students progress, their strengths and weaknesses may change, and their learning plan must adapt accordingly. This flexibility enables educators to provide targeted interventions and personalized instruction, ensuring that students remain engaged and challenged at an appropriate level.

Collaboration among educators, students, and parents is essential for successful continuous assessment and modification of individualized learning plans. Regular communication allows for the exchange of information, feedback, and insights that can inform decision-making. By involving all stakeholders in the process, educators can gather diverse perspectives and implement changes that best support the student's learning journey.

In conclusion, continuously assessing and modifying individualized learning plans is a vital aspect of curriculum development in special education. By regularly evaluating student progress, identifying areas of improvement, and modifying the plan accordingly, educators can ensure that students receive the personalized support they need to thrive. Collaboration and open communication among all stakeholders are key to successful implementation. Ultimately, the goal is to create an inclusive educational environment where every student can reach their full potential.

Transitioning Students to New Curriculum Levels

One of the key challenges in special education is ensuring a smooth transition for students as they progress through different curriculum levels. This subchapter aims to provide valuable insights and strategies for educators, curriculum developers, and anyone interested in the field of curriculum development.

Transitioning students to new curriculum levels is a critical aspect of customized learning, especially in special education. It involves carefully planning and implementing curriculum changes to meet the individual needs of each student. This subchapter will explore various ways to effectively facilitate this transition and support the continuous growth and development of students.

Firstly, it is essential to understand the unique needs and abilities of each student before transitioning them to a new curriculum level. This understanding can be achieved through ongoing assessment and evaluation, allowing educators to identify strengths, weaknesses, and areas requiring additional support. By utilizing this information, curriculum developers can tailor the curriculum to meet the specific learning goals and objectives of each student.

Secondly, collaboration between educators, parents, and other professionals plays a crucial role in successfully transitioning students to new curriculum levels. Regular communication and sharing of information help create a comprehensive support system for students, ensuring a smooth transition. This subchapter will explore effective strategies for developing strong partnerships and fostering open lines of communication among all stakeholders.

Additionally, this subchapter will delve into the importance of providing students with a clear roadmap for their educational journey. Establishing clear learning goals, objectives, and milestones helps students understand what is expected of them and provides a sense of direction. It also allows educators to track progress and make necessary adjustments to the curriculum to ensure continued growth.

Furthermore, this subchapter will explore the significance of incorporating individualized instruction and learning strategies into the curriculum. By considering the unique learning styles and preferences of each student, educators can create a more engaging and effective learning experience. This subchapter will provide practical examples and techniques for implementing individualized instruction in special education curriculum development.

In conclusion, transitioning students to new curriculum levels is a critical aspect of providing customized learning experiences in special education. This subchapter will equip educators, curriculum developers, and anyone interested in curriculum development with valuable insights, strategies, and practical examples to facilitate smooth transitions for students, ultimately supporting their continuous growth and development.

Addressing Post-Secondary Goals and Transition Planning

In the journey of education, the ultimate goal is to equip students with the necessary skills and knowledge to navigate their way through life successfully. This is especially true for students with special education needs, as their unique circumstances require a more tailored approach to curriculum development. In this subchapter titled "Addressing Post-Secondary Goals and Transition Planning," we delve into the crucial aspects of preparing students for life beyond the confines of the classroom.

Transition planning plays a pivotal role in ensuring a smooth and successful transition from the educational setting to post-secondary life. It involves collaborative efforts among educators, families, and community members to identify and address the specific needs and goals of each student. By focusing on individualized transition plans, we can empower students to reach their full potential and achieve greater independence.

One key aspect of transition planning is the identification of post-secondary goals. These goals encompass various areas, including further education, employment, independent living, and community involvement. By setting clear and achievable goals, students can work towards a future that aligns with their interests and aspirations. This process involves assessing their strengths, interests, and preferences, as well as exploring different post-secondary options and opportunities.

To effectively address post-secondary goals, educators must develop a comprehensive curriculum that supports these objectives. Customized learning is an essential approach in special education, as it recognizes the unique needs of each student. By tailoring the curriculum to individual strengths, interests, and learning styles, students are more engaged and motivated to achieve their goals. This approach also fosters a sense of ownership and self-advocacy, empowering students to take an active role in their own education.

Furthermore, successful transition planning requires collaboration and coordination among various stakeholders. Educators, families, community agencies, and employers must work together to provide students with the necessary support and resources. This may include job shadowing opportunities, vocational training programs, internships, and mentorships. By cultivating these partnerships, we can create a seamless transition process that sets students up for success in the post-secondary world.

In conclusion, addressing post-secondary goals and transition planning is crucial for the development of special education curriculum. By focusing on individualized transition plans, setting clear post-secondary goals, and implementing customized learning approaches, we can empower students with special needs to thrive in their chosen paths. Collaboration among educators, families, and community members is key to creating a supportive and inclusive environment that prepares students for a successful transition into post-secondary life.

Chapter 9: Supporting Inclusion and Collaboration

Promoting Inclusive Practices in Special Education Curriculum

In today's diverse society, it is critical to promote inclusive practices in special education curriculum development. Inclusion refers to the idea that all students, regardless of their abilities or disabilities, should have equal opportunities to participate in and benefit from education. By incorporating inclusive practices into the special education curriculum, we can create a more equitable and supportive learning environment for all students.

One of the key aspects of promoting inclusive practices is recognizing the individual needs of students. Each student is unique and has their own strengths, weaknesses, and learning styles. Therefore, it is essential to develop a customized learning plan that caters to their specific needs. This includes considering their academic abilities, social and emotional development, and any additional support they may require. By doing so, we can ensure that every student receives a tailored education that maximizes their potential.

Another important aspect of promoting inclusivity is fostering a sense of belonging and acceptance among students. Inclusive practices involve creating a classroom environment where diversity is celebrated and differences are embraced. This can be achieved through various strategies such as peer support programs, collaborative learning opportunities, and incorporating culturally responsive teaching methods. By encouraging interaction and collaboration among students of different abilities, we can break down barriers and promote social integration.

Furthermore, inclusive practices in special education curriculum development require collaboration and partnership among all stakeholders. This includes educators, parents, administrators, and community members. By involving all these parties in the curriculum development process, we can ensure that the curriculum reflects the needs and aspirations of the students it serves. It is also important to provide ongoing professional development for educators to enhance their knowledge and skills in inclusive teaching practices.

In conclusion, promoting inclusive practices in special education curriculum development is essential for creating a supportive and equitable learning environment for all students. By recognizing individual needs, fostering a sense of belonging, and fostering collaboration among stakeholders, we can develop a curriculum that meets the diverse needs of students with disabilities. Inclusion is not only a legal requirement but also a moral and ethical imperative. By embracing inclusive practices, we can empower students with disabilities to reach their full potential and contribute meaningfully to society.

Collaborating with General Education Teachers for Integrated Learning

In the ever-evolving landscape of education, the demand for inclusive and individualized learning experiences has become increasingly important. As educators, we strive to meet the unique needs of every student, including those with special education requirements. One powerful approach to achieving this goal is through the collaboration between special education teachers and general education teachers.

The concept of integrated learning holds significant potential for creating a comprehensive and inclusive educational environment. By combining the expertise and resources of both special education and general education teachers, we can design a curriculum that addresses the diverse needs of all students.

Collaboration between general education and special education teachers is not only beneficial for students with special needs but for all students. Integrated learning promotes an inclusive classroom environment where students can learn from each other, fostering empathy and understanding. It enables educators to provide differentiated instruction that caters to individual learning styles and abilities, ensuring that no student is left behind.

To effectively collaborate with general education teachers, special education teachers must communicate openly and establish a shared vision for instruction. This involves regular meetings, brainstorming sessions, and the development of common goals and objectives. By working together, educators can identify areas where students with special needs can actively participate in the general education curriculum, while also receiving the additional support they require.

Special education teachers can contribute valuable insights to curriculum development by providing strategies and accommodations that benefit all students. By adapting existing materials and resources, educators can create inclusive lesson plans that incorporate different learning modalities, promote critical thinking, and enhance student engagement.

Furthermore, collaboration between special education and general education teachers can extend beyond the classroom. By sharing knowledge and experiences, educators can create a supportive network that fosters professional growth and development. This collaboration can also lead to the identification and implementation of innovative teaching practices, ensuring that curriculum development remains dynamic and responsive to the changing needs of students.

In conclusion, collaborating with general education teachers for integrated learning is a powerful approach to developing a specialized curriculum for individual needs. By tapping into the collective expertise and resources of both special education and general education teachers, we can create an inclusive learning environment that benefits all students. This collaboration not only enhances the educational experience for students with special needs but also promotes empathy, understanding, and growth for all learners. Together, we can move towards a future where every student receives the education they deserve.

Enhancing Peer Interactions and Social Skills Development

In today's inclusive educational environments, it is crucial to prioritize the development of peer interactions and social skills for students with special needs. The ability to form positive relationships with peers not only enhances their social well-being but also plays a significant role in their academic success. This subchapter aims to provide valuable insights and strategies for curriculum development professionals on how to effectively enhance peer interactions and foster social skills development within the special education curriculum.

Creating an inclusive classroom environment is the first step towards promoting positive peer interactions. By incorporating collaborative learning activities and group projects, students are given opportunities to interact and work together. This promotes the development of essential social skills such as communication, cooperation, and problem-solving. Teachers can also implement structured activities that encourage peer interactions, such as partner work or small group discussions. These activities provide a safe and supportive space for students to practice social skills and build relationships.

Another important aspect of enhancing peer interactions is explicitly teaching social skills. Incorporating social skills training into the curriculum helps students understand and practice appropriate social behaviors. This can be achieved through various methods such as role-playing, modeling, and guided practice. Teachers can also incorporate social stories or video modeling to teach social skills in a visual and engaging manner. By consistently reinforcing and practicing these skills, students will gradually internalize them and apply them in real-life situations.

Furthermore, peer mentoring programs can be implemented to foster positive peer interactions. Pairing students with special needs with typically developing peers creates opportunities for meaningful connections to be formed. This not only benefits students with special needs by providing them with role models and support, but it also promotes empathy and understanding among their peers.

Lastly, it is essential to regularly assess and monitor students' progress in peer interactions and social skills development. This can be done through observation, self-assessment, or peer feedback. By tracking progress, teachers can identify areas that need additional support and tailor instructional strategies accordingly.

In conclusion, enhancing peer interactions and social skills development is crucial in the special education curriculum. By creating an inclusive environment, teaching social skills explicitly, implementing peer mentoring programs, and monitoring progress, curriculum development professionals can ensure that students with special needs have the necessary tools to thrive socially and academically. Ultimately, by prioritizing peer interactions and social skills development, we are fostering a more inclusive and supportive educational environment for all students.

Chapter 10: Addressing Behavioral and Emotional Needs

Understanding the Impact of Behavior on Learning

In the ever-evolving field of curriculum development, it is essential to recognize and address the impact of behavior on learning. Behavior plays a crucial role in the educational journey of every individual, particularly in the realm of special education. To successfully develop a specialized curriculum for students with individual needs, it is vital to understand how behavior can both positively and negatively affect the learning process.

Behavioral challenges can significantly hinder a student's ability to engage and progress academically. These challenges may manifest as disruptive behavior, difficulty following instructions, or an inability to concentrate for extended periods. In some cases, students may exhibit behavior that is a direct result of their struggles with certain subjects or tasks. Consequently, their negative behavior can create barriers to effective learning.

Conversely, positive behavior can greatly enhance the learning experience for students. When students are motivated, engaged, and exhibit good behavior, they are more likely to absorb information, actively participate in classroom activities, and achieve better academic outcomes. Recognizing and reinforcing positive behavior can create a positive feedback loop, fostering a conducive learning environment for all students.

To address the impact of behavior on learning, a customized curriculum should incorporate strategies to support students with diverse behavioral needs. This may involve implementing behavior management techniques, providing individualized attention, and fostering a positive and inclusive classroom culture. Additionally, educators should collaborate with other professionals, such as psychologists or behavior specialists, to develop tailored interventions and support plans for students with challenging behaviors.

It is important to remember that behavior is influenced by various factors, including a student's personal experiences, environment, and emotional well-being. Therefore, a comprehensive approach to curriculum development should also consider these factors. Creating a safe and supportive environment, establishing clear expectations and routines, and promoting social-emotional development can contribute to positive behavior and improved learning outcomes.

In conclusion, understanding the impact of behavior on learning is crucial in the realm of curriculum development, especially in special education. By recognizing the influence of both positive and negative behavior on the learning process, educators can design customized curricula that address individual needs effectively. Through the implementation of appropriate behavior management techniques and support plans, educators can foster a conducive learning environment that empowers students to reach their full potential.

Implementing Positive Behavior Supports in the Curriculum

Positive behavior supports play a crucial role in creating an inclusive and nurturing learning environment for students with special needs. By integrating these supports into the curriculum, educators can ensure that students receive the necessary tools and strategies to succeed academically and socially. This subchapter explores the various ways in which positive behavior supports can be implemented in the curriculum, emphasizing the importance of customized learning for individual needs.

One of the key aspects of implementing positive behavior supports in the curriculum is fostering a positive and respectful classroom culture. Educators should focus on creating a safe and supportive environment where students feel valued and accepted. This can be achieved through the use of collaborative learning strategies, promoting empathy and understanding among students.

Additionally, incorporating explicit teaching of social and emotional skills into the curriculum is essential. By explicitly teaching skills such as self-regulation, problem-solving, and empathy, students can develop the necessary tools to navigate social interactions and regulate their emotions effectively. These skills can be integrated into various subject areas, such as language arts, math, and science, to ensure holistic development.

Furthermore, individualized behavior plans should be created to address the specific needs of each student. These plans can be developed collaboratively with the student, their parents, and other professionals involved in their education. By tailoring the curriculum to meet the individual needs of each student, educators can provide targeted supports and accommodations to promote their success.

Another crucial aspect of implementing positive behavior supports in the curriculum is the use of positive reinforcement. Educators should focus on recognizing and rewarding positive behavior, fostering a sense of motivation and engagement among students. This can be achieved through various strategies such as verbal praise, tangible rewards, and privilege systems.

Lastly, ongoing professional development for educators is essential to ensure the effective implementation of positive behavior supports in the curriculum. By providing educators with the necessary training and resources, they can enhance their knowledge and skills in supporting students with special needs. Collaboration and communication among educators, parents, and other stakeholders are also vital in creating a cohesive and supportive learning environment.

In conclusion, implementing positive behavior supports in the curriculum is crucial for the success of students with special needs. By fostering a positive classroom culture, teaching social and emotional skills, creating individualized behavior plans, utilizing positive reinforcement, and providing ongoing professional development, educators can create a customized learning experience that meets the individual needs of each student. This subchapter aims to equip educators with practical strategies to implement positive behavior supports effectively, promoting inclusive and supportive learning environments for all students.

Supporting Emotional Regulation and Mental Health

In today's rapidly changing world, it is more important than ever to prioritize emotional regulation and mental health for individuals of all ages. This is especially true within the context of curriculum development, as education plays a crucial role in shaping the overall well-being of students. In this subchapter, we will delve into the significance of supporting emotional regulation and mental health in the development of specialized education curriculum tailored to individual needs.

Emotional regulation refers to the ability to manage and express emotions in a healthy and constructive manner. It is a vital skill that allows individuals to navigate through life's challenges and build resilience. By incorporating strategies to support emotional regulation within the curriculum, educators can create a safe and supportive environment for students to explore and understand their emotions.

One effective approach to supporting emotional regulation is through the implementation of social-emotional learning (SEL) programs. These programs provide students with the necessary tools and skills to recognize and regulate their emotions, develop empathy, and build positive relationships. By integrating SEL into the curriculum, educators can promote emotional well-being and foster a positive classroom climate.

Furthermore, mental health should be a key consideration when developing specialized education curriculum. Mental health issues such as anxiety, depression, and attention deficit hyperactivity disorder (ADHD) can significantly impact a student's ability to learn and succeed academically. By addressing mental health needs within the curriculum, educators can provide necessary support and accommodations to ensure students' overall well-being.

Incorporating mindfulness practices into the curriculum is another effective way to support mental health. Mindfulness exercises, such as deep breathing and meditation, can help students reduce stress, improve concentration, and enhance self-awareness. By dedicating time to mindfulness activities, educators can empower students to better manage their mental health and navigate through academic challenges.

In conclusion, supporting emotional regulation and mental health is crucial in the development of specialized education curriculum for individual needs. By prioritizing emotional well-being, educators can create a nurturing environment that promotes positive social-emotional development and resilience. Similarly, addressing mental health needs within the curriculum ensures that students receive the necessary support to thrive academically and personally. As curriculum developers, it is our responsibility to ensure that emotional regulation and mental health are integral components of educational programs, enabling all learners to reach their full potential.

Chapter 11: Professional Development and Training

Providing Professional Development for Special Education Teachers

Special education teachers play a crucial role in the lives of students with diverse learning needs. To ensure that these educators are equipped with the necessary skills and knowledge to support their students effectively, professional development opportunities are essential. This subchapter explores the importance of providing professional development specifically tailored for special education teachers and how it contributes to customized learning.

Professional development for special education teachers encompasses a wide range of activities, including workshops, conferences, seminars, and ongoing training sessions. These opportunities aim to enhance teachers' understanding of special education laws, teaching strategies, assessment techniques, and the use of assistive technology. By staying up-to-date with the latest research and best practices, special education teachers can create a dynamic and inclusive learning environment for their students.

One key aspect of professional development for special education teachers is the emphasis on individualized instruction. As the book "Customized Learning: Developing Special Education Curriculum for Individual Needs" highlights, each student has unique learning requirements. Therefore, special education teachers must be equipped with the skills to create personalized curriculum plans that address these individual needs effectively. Professional development opportunities provide teachers with the tools and strategies to tailor instruction, modify assessments, and differentiate materials to ensure that every student can thrive academically.

Furthermore, professional development also promotes collaboration among special education teachers and other professionals, such as general education teachers, therapists, and administrators. By fostering a collaborative environment, teachers can share their experiences, exchange ideas, and learn from one another. This collaboration enhances their ability to address complex challenges and develop innovative approaches to teaching students with special needs.

In conclusion, providing professional development specifically designed for special education teachers is vital for the successful implementation of customized learning. These opportunities empower teachers with the knowledge, skills, and resources necessary to create individualized curriculum plans and effectively support students with diverse learning needs. By investing in the professional growth of special education teachers, we can ensure that every student receives an inclusive education that maximizes their potential. This subchapter aims to inform educators, curriculum developers, and anyone interested in special education about the importance of professional development and its impact on creating a conducive learning environment for students with special needs.

Building the Capacity of School Staff to Implement Individualized Learning

In today's educational landscape, it is imperative that school staff possess the necessary skills to implement individualized learning effectively. Individualized learning recognizes that every student has unique needs, strengths, and learning styles, and aims to tailor instruction to meet these individual requirements. To achieve this, it is crucial to build the capacity of school staff, empowering them to support students with diverse learning needs effectively.

The process of building staff capacity begins with professional development opportunities that focus on curriculum development. This subchapter will explore various strategies and techniques that school staff can employ to create customized learning experiences for students with special education needs.

One approach to building staff capacity is through understanding and implementing Universal Design for Learning (UDL) principles. UDL promotes the creation of flexible learning environments that can be accessed by all students, regardless of their abilities or disabilities. By familiarizing staff with UDL principles, they can make informed decisions about curriculum design, instructional methods, and assessment strategies that cater to individual student needs.

Another critical aspect of capacity building is providing ongoing support and training to school staff. This could include workshops, mentoring programs, and collaborative learning opportunities. By fostering a culture of continuous professional development, schools can ensure that staff remain up-to-date with best practices in individualized learning and are equipped with the necessary tools to implement them effectively.

Furthermore, it is vital to foster a collaborative and inclusive school culture that values the expertise and contributions of all staff members. By encouraging open communication and collaboration among teachers, special education professionals, and support staff, schools can create a cohesive team that works together to support individualized learning initiatives.

Lastly, technology can play a significant role in building staff capacity. Integrating educational technology tools and resources into the curriculum can enhance individualized learning experiences, provide personalized feedback, and facilitate data-driven decision-making. School staff should be trained on how to effectively utilize technology to support individual student needs and ensure they are equipped with the necessary skills to navigate and leverage digital resources.

In conclusion, building the capacity of school staff to implement individualized learning is essential for providing quality education to all students, particularly those with special education needs. By focusing on professional development, ongoing support, collaboration, and the integration of technology, schools can empower their staff to create customized learning experiences that meet the unique needs of every student.

Staying Up-to-Date with Best Practices in Special Education Curriculum

In the rapidly evolving field of special education, it is crucial for educators and curriculum developers to stay up-to-date with the best practices in designing and implementing specialized curriculum. With the diverse and unique needs of individual students, it is necessary to continuously adapt and refine curriculum strategies to provide the most effective learning experiences. This subchapter aims to guide curriculum developers and educators in their pursuit of staying current with the latest trends and research in special education curriculum development.

One of the most effective ways to stay up-to-date with best practices is to engage in ongoing professional development opportunities. Attending workshops, conferences, and seminars that focus on special education curriculum development can provide invaluable insights into emerging practices and evidence-based strategies. These events offer opportunities for networking, collaboration, and sharing of ideas, allowing educators to learn from one another's experiences and expertise.

Additionally, subscribing to professional journals and publications in the field of special education can provide a wealth of information on the latest research, trends, and best practices. Reading articles written by experts and practitioners in the field can help educators gain a deeper understanding of successful curriculum development approaches. Online resources, such as blogs and websites dedicated to special education, can also be a valuable source of information and inspiration.

Collaboration with other educators and curriculum developers is another powerful tool for staying up-to-date with best practices. Joining professional organizations and participating in online forums or discussion groups can provide a platform for sharing ideas, asking questions, and engaging in meaningful conversations about special education curriculum. By collaborating with others, educators can gain different perspectives and insights into effective strategies, leading to more comprehensive and inclusive curriculum design.

Finally, staying connected with the broader educational community is essential for staying up-to-date with best practices in special education curriculum. Engaging in dialogues with administrators, parents, and students can provide valuable feedback and insights into the effectiveness of current curriculum strategies. Regularly seeking input from stakeholders and incorporating their perspectives into curriculum development can lead to more student-centered and inclusive practices.

In conclusion, staying up-to-date with best practices in special education curriculum development is crucial for educators and curriculum developers. Ongoing professional development, reading research articles, collaborating with others, and engaging with stakeholders are key strategies for remaining current in this rapidly evolving field. By continuously striving to improve and adapt curriculum strategies, educators can ensure that they are providing the most effective and inclusive learning experiences for students with special needs.

Chapter 12: Case Studies and Success Stories

Real-Life Examples of Individualized Learning Success

In today's rapidly changing educational landscape, the concept of individualized learning has gained significant attention and recognition. As educators strive to meet the diverse needs of students, the implementation of customized learning approaches has become increasingly crucial. This subchapter aims to provide real-life examples of individualized learning success, showcasing the positive impact it can have on students of all abilities.

One inspiring example of individualized learning success is the story of Sarah, a fourth-grade student with dyslexia. Sarah struggled with reading and writing, often feeling frustrated and discouraged. However, her teacher recognized her unique learning needs and developed a personalized curriculum to address them. By incorporating multisensory teaching methods and providing additional resources, Sarah's confidence and abilities began to soar. Today, Sarah is not only reading fluently but has also discovered a passion for creative writing, demonstrating that personalized instruction can unlock hidden talents and unleash the full potential of students.

Another remarkable instance of individualized learning success is the case of Michael, a high school student diagnosed with autism spectrum disorder. Traditional classroom settings posed significant challenges for Michael, as he often experienced sensory overload and struggled with social interactions. In response, his school adopted a customized learning approach, allowing Michael to engage in hands-on, project-based learning activities while providing him with a quiet and supportive environment. This tailored approach not only enhanced Michael's academic performance but also fostered his social and emotional growth, enabling him to develop meaningful relationships with peers and thrive in a school setting.

These real-life examples highlight the power of individualized learning in transforming the educational experiences of students. By recognizing and addressing the unique needs of each learner, educators can create an inclusive and supportive learning environment that fosters success for all students, regardless of their abilities or challenges.

Implementing individualized learning approaches in curriculum development not only benefits students with special needs but also enhances the educational experience for all learners. By embracing customized learning, educators can design curriculum frameworks that cater to the diverse learning styles, strengths, and interests of their students. This approach encourages active participation, promotes critical thinking, and fosters a love for lifelong learning.

In conclusion, the real-life examples of Sarah and Michael exemplify the transformative power of individualized learning. By personalizing instruction, educators can create an environment where all students can thrive academically, socially, and emotionally. As curriculum developers, it is essential to consider the diverse needs of learners and embrace customized learning approaches to unlock the full potential of every student.

Showcasing Effective Special Education Curriculum Development

In the realm of education, the importance of providing inclusive and individualized learning experiences for students with special needs cannot be overstated. It is crucial to develop a curriculum that caters to their unique requirements, ensuring that they receive the necessary support and opportunities to thrive academically and socially. This subchapter aims to shed light on the significance of effective special education curriculum development and how it can positively impact students with diverse learning needs.

Special education curriculum development involves creating and implementing tailored instructional plans that address the specific strengths, weaknesses, and learning styles of each student. It goes beyond merely adapting general education materials; instead, it focuses on designing a curriculum that fosters meaningful engagement, promotes skill development, and enhances overall learning outcomes. By showcasing effective practices in this domain, we aim to inspire curriculum developers, educators, and stakeholders to embrace a more personalized approach to education.

One key aspect of effective special education curriculum development is the use of evidence-based strategies. Drawing on research-backed methodologies, educators can ensure that the curriculum is grounded in sound pedagogical principles and best practices. This includes employing differentiated instruction techniques, multisensory approaches, assistive technology, and adaptive materials to accommodate diverse learning needs. By incorporating these strategies, educators can create an inclusive learning environment that caters to students' individual strengths and needs.

Furthermore, collaboration plays a vital role in developing an effective special education curriculum. It is essential for curriculum developers, educators, parents, and specialists to work together as a team, leveraging their expertise and insights to design a comprehensive and cohesive curriculum. By fostering a collaborative approach, we can tap into a wealth of knowledge and experiences, leading to the creation of a curriculum that truly meets the unique requirements of each student.

To showcase effective special education curriculum development, this subchapter will provide case studies, success stories, and practical examples from educators and experts in the field. These real-life examples will highlight the positive impact of customized learning on students' academic progress, self-esteem, and overall well-being. By delving into these stories, readers will gain a deeper understanding of the transformative power of personalized education and be inspired to advocate for its implementation in their own educational settings.

In conclusion, effective special education curriculum development is essential for promoting inclusive and individualized learning experiences for students with diverse learning needs. By showcasing evidence-based strategies and fostering collaboration, we can design a curriculum that caters to each student's unique strengths and challenges, enabling them to reach their full potential. This subchapter aims to inspire curriculum developers, educators, and stakeholders to embrace a more personalized approach to education, ultimately benefiting students with special needs and creating a more inclusive educational landscape for all.

Lessons Learned and Future Directions

In the ever-evolving field of special education curriculum development, continuous learning and adaptation are essential. The journey toward customized learning for individual needs has taught us valuable lessons and provided insights into future directions that can further enhance the educational experience for all learners.

One of the primary lessons learned is the importance of embracing diversity and inclusivity. Recognizing that each learner has unique abilities, strengths, and challenges is crucial in designing customized learning experiences. By valuing diversity, we can create a curriculum that addresses the specific needs of every student, ensuring that no one is left behind.

Another lesson we have learned is the significance of collaboration and teamwork. Developing a special education curriculum requires input from various stakeholders, including educators, parents, therapists, and administrators. By fostering a collaborative environment, we can pool our collective expertise and experiences to create a curriculum that truly meets the individual needs of students.

Furthermore, the integration of technology has proven to be a game-changer in special education curriculum development. Technology provides new opportunities for personalized learning, allowing students to access content at their own pace and in a format that suits their learning style. By leveraging technology, we can ensure that every learner has equal access to quality education.

Looking ahead, there are several future directions that hold immense potential for advancing customized learning in special education. One such direction is the integration of artificial intelligence (AI) and machine learning algorithms. With AI, we can develop adaptive learning systems that analyze student performance and tailor instruction to their specific needs in real-time. This personalized approach can significantly enhance the learning outcomes for students with special needs.

Another future direction is the expansion of community partnerships. Collaborating with community organizations, businesses, and professionals can provide valuable resources and opportunities for students with special needs. By forging these partnerships, we can create a curriculum that incorporates real-world experiences and fosters the development of essential life skills.

In conclusion, the lessons learned and future directions in special education curriculum development emphasize the importance of embracing diversity, fostering collaboration, and leveraging technology. By continuously evolving our approach and incorporating innovative strategies, we can ensure that every learner receives a customized education that caters to their individual needs. Together, let us strive towards a future where all students, regardless of their abilities, have equal opportunities to thrive and succeed.

Conclusion: Embracing Customized Learning for All Students

In today's rapidly evolving education landscape, it is more important than ever to embrace customized learning for all students. The traditional one-size-fits-all approach to education is no longer sufficient in meeting the diverse needs of students with special education requirements. As curriculum developers, it is our responsibility to ensure that every student has access to a tailored education that meets their individual needs and maximizes their potential.

Customized learning recognizes that each student is unique, with their own set of strengths, weaknesses, and learning styles. By adopting this approach, we can create a more inclusive and empowering educational environment that allows all students to thrive. Through personalized learning plans, individualized instruction, and adaptive technologies, we can ensure that every student receives the support and resources they need to succeed academically, socially, and emotionally.

One of the key benefits of customized learning is its ability to foster a sense of ownership and engagement among students. When students feel that their education is tailored to their specific needs and interests, they are more likely to be motivated and actively participate in their learning journey. This personalized approach also promotes a deeper understanding of the subject matter, as it allows students to explore concepts at their own pace and in a way that resonates with them.

Furthermore, customized learning allows for a more holistic approach to education. By considering the individual needs of students, we can design curricula that not only focus on academic skills but also address their social, emotional, and behavioral development. This comprehensive approach ensures that students are equipped with the necessary skills and competencies to navigate the challenges of the real world successfully.

Implementing customized learning requires a collaborative effort from educators, administrators, parents, and the wider community. It is essential to promote a culture of inclusivity and support, where everyone understands the importance of personalized education for students with special needs. By working together, we can create an educational system that empowers every student to reach their full potential.

In conclusion, embracing customized learning for all students is a crucial step towards creating an inclusive and empowering educational environment. By tailoring education to individual needs, we can foster engagement, promote deeper understanding, and develop well-rounded individuals. As curriculum developers, it is our responsibility to advocate for and implement customized learning practices to ensure that every student has equal access to a high-quality education. By doing so, we can create a brighter future for all students, regardless of their unique learning requirements.

www.ingramcontent.com/pod-product-compliance
Lightning Source LLC
Chambersburg PA
CBHW051345150726
48000CB00003B/1052